# MY ALLAH SERIES

## ALLAH CREATED COLORS

### KISA KIDS PUBLICATIONS

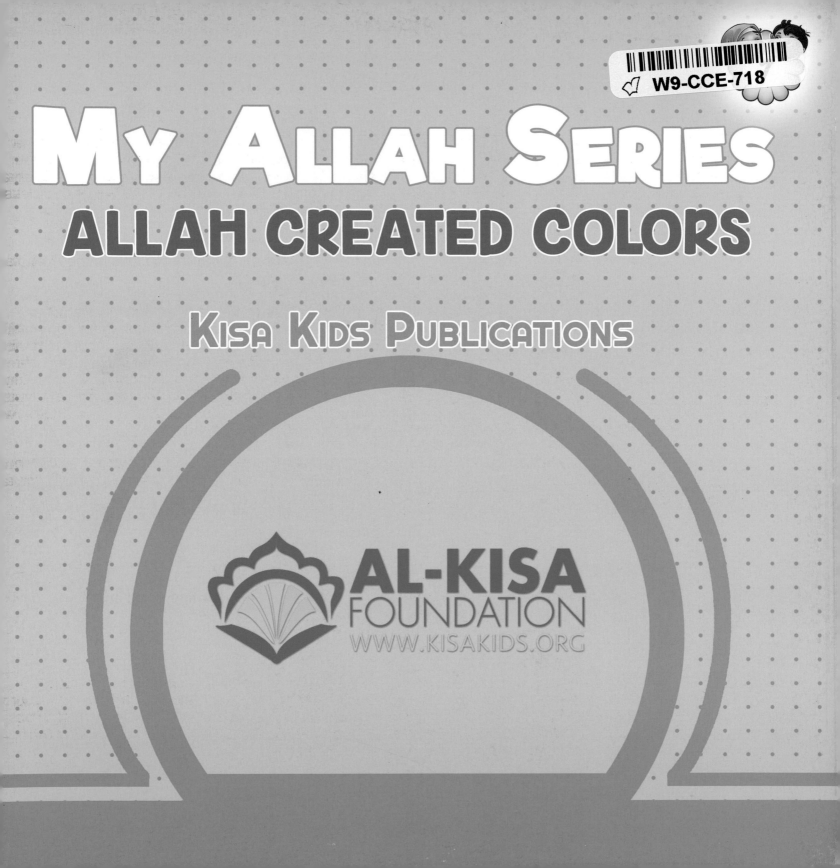

**AL-KISA**
FOUNDATION
WWW.KISAKIDS.ORG

# PARENTS' CORNER

صِبْغَةَ اللَّـهِ وَمَنْ أَحْسَنُ مِنَ اللَّـهِ صِبْغَةً

*Adopt the color of Allāh, and who is better than Allāh in coloring?*
(Sūrat al-Baqarah, Verse 138)

Dear Parents/Guardians,

Children love Allāh and desperately want to know who He is. The concept of the unseen is impossible for young children to grasp, so they ask questions such as, "Where is Allāh? Where does He live? What does He eat?" Even though these questions are difficult to answer and put parents in a tough situation, we need to see and understand these questions for what they truly are: blessings. Through these questions, we can see how children have a special place for Allāh in their hearts and would like to know more about Him.

According to aḥadīth, the heart is the ḥaram (sacred place) of Allāh. Therefore, one way to answer these questions is to let children know that Allāh is with us all the time. The more good deeds we do and good choices we make, the closer we get to Allāh. Because Allāh is innately embedded in their tiny hearts and souls, they will feel the goodness and "warmth" of Allāh's love whenever they make good choices. This, in turn, will give them peace and a feeling of contentment which will satisfy them, even if they don't get the exact answers to their questions.

Allāh says in the Quran, "Adopt the color of Allāh, and who is better than Allāh in coloring?" This "color" represents our good deeds and the closeness our hearts feel to Allāh. When someone's entire being thinks, feels, and acts in a manner that is pleasing to Allāh, they are exhibiting this color.

*Allah Created Colors* highlights the fact that Allāh doesn't have a primary or secondary color. However, a child can adapt Allāh's color through their actions and behavior. InshaAllāh, while reading this book, we pray your children can strengthen their connection to Allāh by trying to attain His color in their hearts.

With Duʿas,
Kisa Kids Publications

Look at the tall green trees, sweet red roses, and clouds that are white.
This world is full of colors that are so beautiful and bright.

*What are some other colors that Allah has created?*

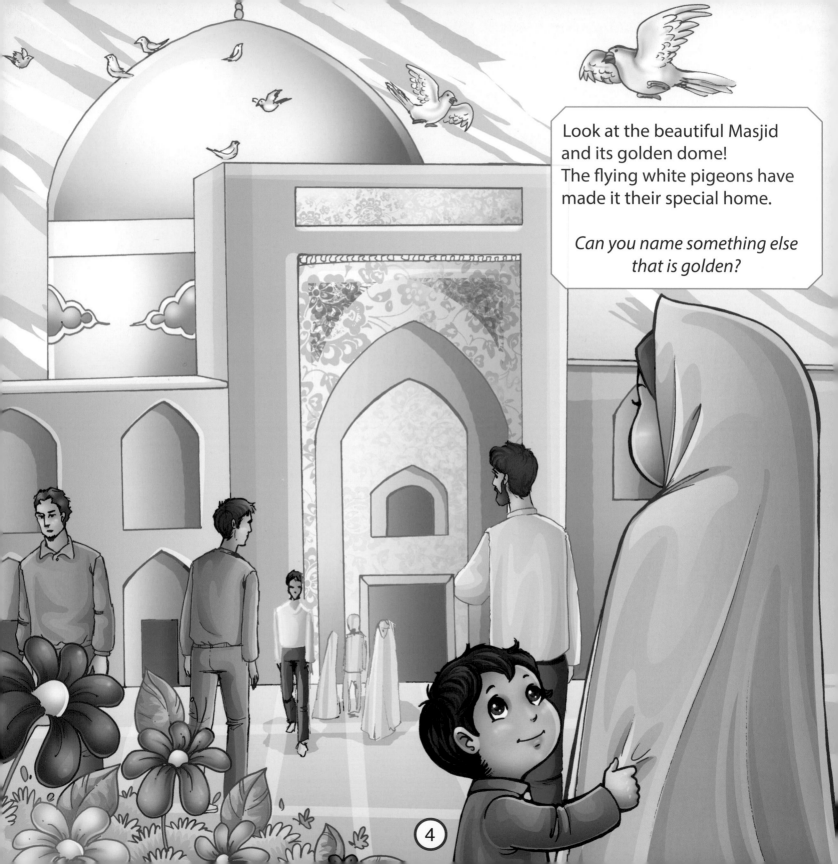

Look at the beautiful Masjid and its golden dome! The flying white pigeons have made it their special home.

*Can you name something else that is golden?*

4

Look at this new tricycle with its bright orange shine. Watch the yellow balloon following closely behind!

*What other colors do you see on this page?*

We see colors all around us like red, blue, and green.
But is there a color for things that cannot be seen?

*Can we see the color if someone is kind or mean?*

Mama gives a loving hug to her dear boy.
But what is the color of their love and joy?

*What are the ways that your Mama shows she loves you?*

The sweet girl sits on the swing and reads her favorite book.
But can you see the color of her learning when you look?

*Does "thinking" have a color?*

Everything that is invisible has no color for us to see.
Allah has no color because He cannot be seen by you and me.
He is the Creator of all the beautiful colors we can see.
But the Quran tells us about another color for you and me.
One that is special and not like the many other colors we see.

It is Allah's special color that comes from faith, imaan, and good deeds. Like the little girl thinking about the Quran as her grandmother reads.

You make Allah happy when you help your Mama.
Like when you set the table for her and Baba.
These good actions will give you a special feeling.
It's Allah's special color you are receiving!

*Can you remember a time that you felt this special color?*

You make Allah so happy when you race to help each other.
When you obey and follow Him, you earn His special color.
"O Allah! Please, always help me to do good deeds.
Fill my heart with Your love and the color it needs!"

*What good deeds have you done?*